CAMBRIDGE
UNIVERSITY PRESS

CAMBRIDGE
Global English Starters

Fun with Letters and Sounds A

Gabrielle Pritchard

My Fun with Letters
and Sounds book

Cambridge Global English Starters **Fun with Letters and Sounds A Pre-writing practice**

1 Join the images.

2 Trace and join.

3 Find the way to the picnic. Draw.

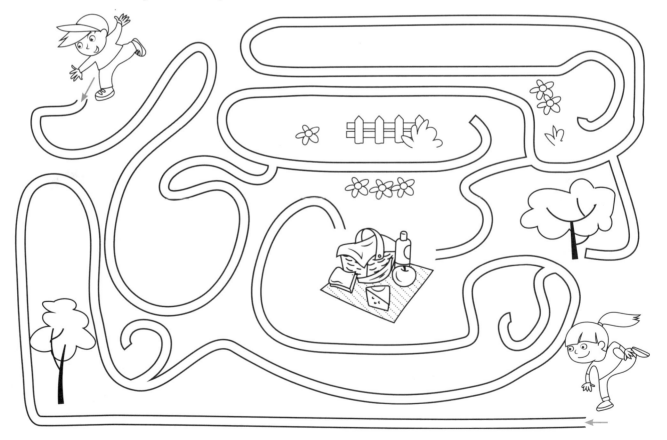

Cambridge Global English Starters **Fun with Letters and Sounds A Pre-writing practice**

4 Complete the picture.

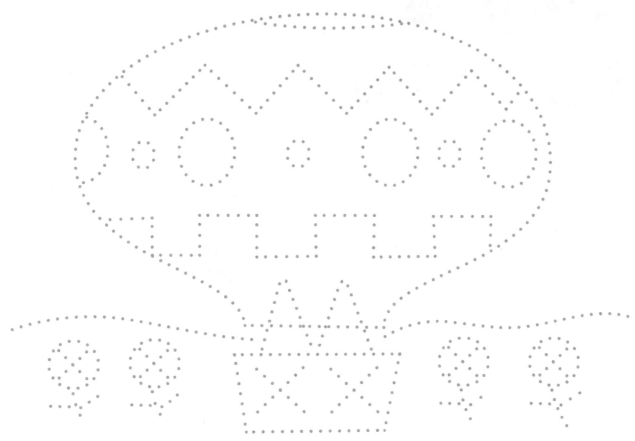

5 Trace O and X. Then play the game.

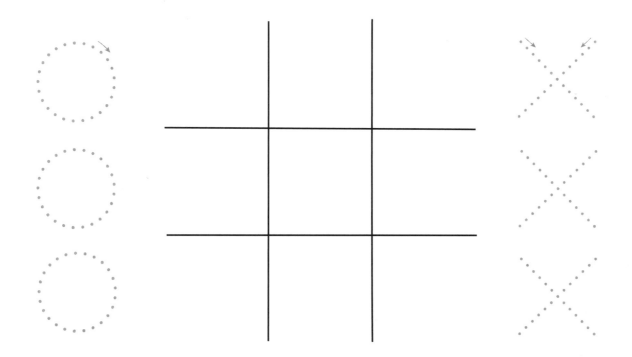

1 Let's learn our letters

 1 Listen and trace.

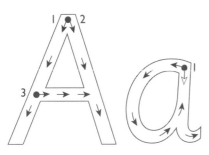   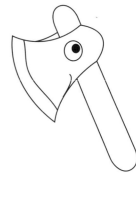

 2a Listen, point and say.

 2b Listen, find and say.

3 Trace and write.

4 ▲▲ Write.

5 Find and trace **A** and **a**.

A c A E a A b
    a c a E a c
a A O a a o C E

6 Colour the things beginning with **A**.
Point and say.

7 🔺 Look, choose and write.

ant   axe   apple
axe   apple   ant
apple   ant   axe

2 Let's learn our letters

 1 Listen and trace.

 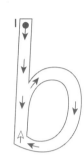   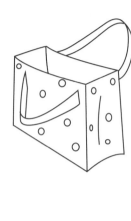

 2a Listen, point and say.

 2b Listen, find and say.

3 Trace and write.

4 ⛰ Write.

B B B

b b b

5 Find and circle **B** and **b.**
Then trace.

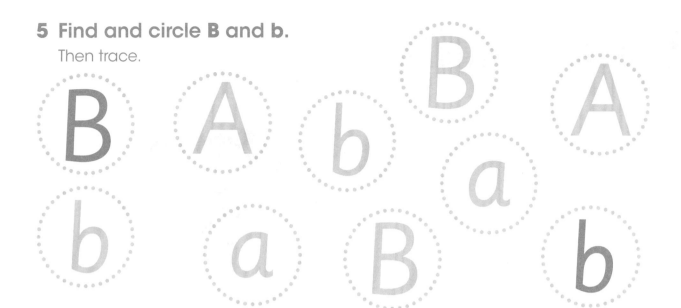

6 Look and tick ✓ **a** or **b.**
Then say.

7 🔺 Match and write.

book   bag   boy

3 Let's learn our letters

 1 Listen and trace.

 2a Listen, point and say.

 2b Listen, find and say.

3 Trace and write.

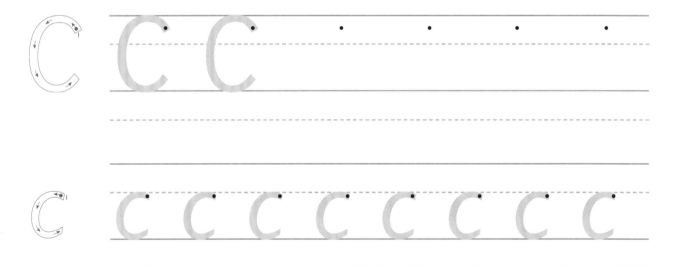

4 ▲▲ Write.

5 Find and colour **A**, **a**, **B**, **b** and **C**, **c**.

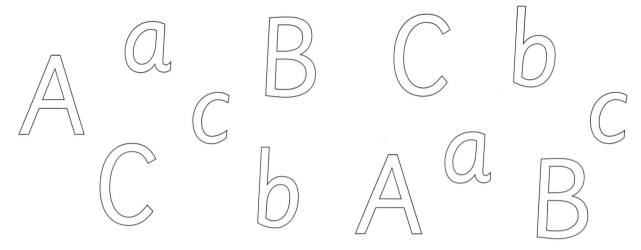

6 Join the dots.

Write **a**, **b** or **c**. Then say.

7 🔺 Look and write.

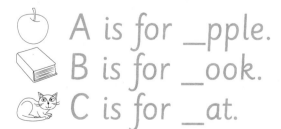

A is for _pple.
B is for _ook.
C is for _at.

4 Story time: The ant and the apple

 1 Listen and point.

 2 ⇅ Listen, say and circle or write.

The ant sees an apple.

The cat sees the ant.

The boy sees the cat.

The cat sees the cow.

Moo!

The cow sees the cat.

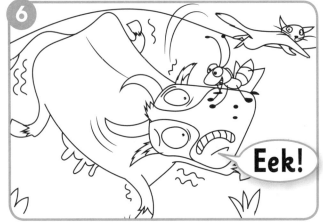

Eek!

The cow sees the ant. Oh no!

3 Colour the animals in the story.

5 I can do it!

1 Listen and colour.
Listen and write **a**, **b** or **c**.

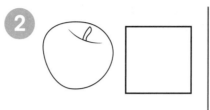

2 Draw lines to match the letters.

A   c   **B**   **A**

B   b   **a**   **b**

C   a   **C**   **c**

3 Match the pictures that start with the same sound.

axe

bag

cow

ant

cap

boy

4 ▲▲ Say and write the words in activity 3.

13

Unit 2

1 Let's learn our letters

 13 **1** Listen and trace.

 14 **2a** Listen, point and say.

 15 **2b** Listen, find and say.

3 Trace and write.

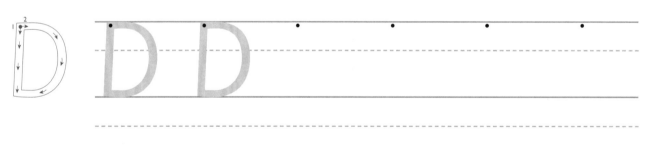

4 🔺 Write.

5 Find and trace **D** and **d**.

D b b d P D P D
b h D h d P b
P h d

6 Colour the things beginning with **D**.

Point and say.

7 Look, choose and write.

den
doll
duck

duck
den
doll

doll
duck
den

2 Let's learn our letters

 1 Listen and trace.

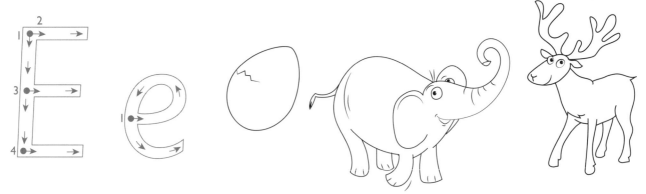

 2a Listen, point and say.

 2b Listen, find and say.

3 Trace and write.

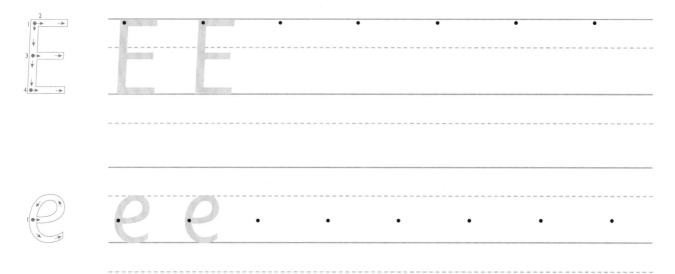

4 ⛰ Write.

5 Find and circle E and e.
Then trace.

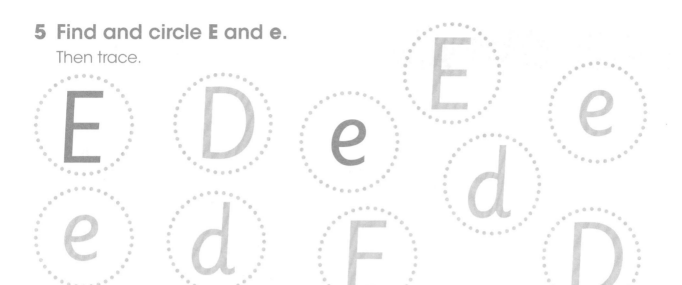

6 Look and tick ✓ d or e.
Then say.

7 🔺 **Match and write.**

egg   elephant   elk

1 Listen and trace.

 2a Listen, point and say.

 2b Listen, find and say.

3 Trace and write.

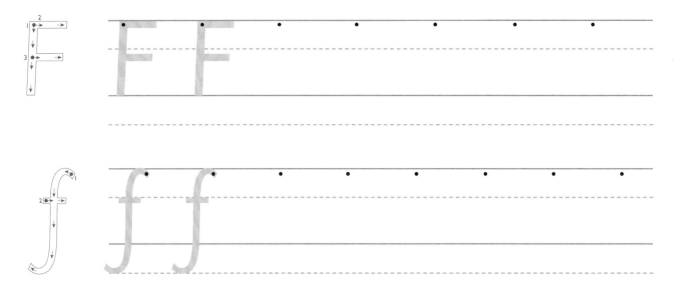

4 ⛰ Write.

5 Find and colour **D**, **d**, **E**, **e** and **F**, **f**.

6 Join the dots.
Write **d**, **e** or **f**. Then say.

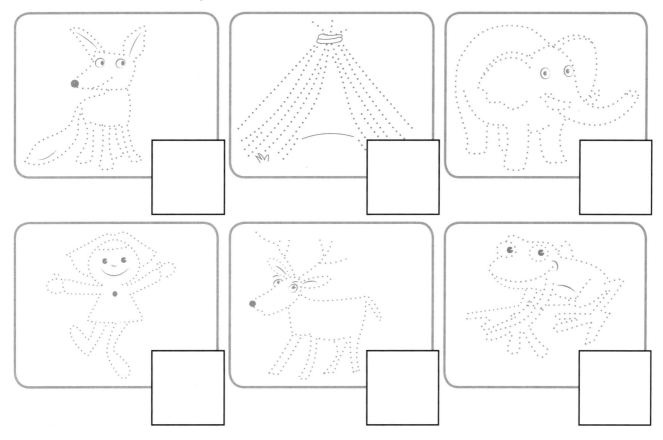

7 🔺 Look and write.

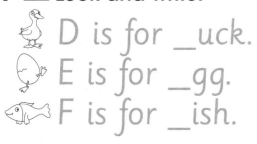
D is for _uck.
E is for _gg.
F is for _ish.

4 Story time: Who's got a den?

 1 Listen and point.

 2 ↕ Listen, say and circle or write.

Look! Fox has got a den.

Elephant has got a den.

Duck and the egg have got a den.

Frog has got a den.

Wow! Fish has got a den, too.

Everyone has got a den!

3 Trace the animals from the sentences.

5 I can do it!

 1 Listen and colour.

Listen and write **d**, **e** or **f**.

2 Draw lines to match the letters.

d   F   **D**   **F**

e   D   **f**   **e**

f   E   **E**   **d**

3 Match the pictures that start with the same sound.

den   elephant   frog

fox   doll   elk

4 ▲▲ **Say and write the words in activity 3.**

21

1 Let's learn our letters

25 **1** Listen and trace.

26 **2a** Listen, point and say.

27 **2b** Listen, find and say.

3 Trace and write.

4 ▲ Write.

5 Find and trace **G** and **g**.

G   f   D   G   G   g   G

g   G   b   g   D   b   f   g

6 Colour the things beginning with **G**.

Point and say.

7 🔺 Look, choose and write.

girl   guitar   goat

guitar   goat   girl

goat   girl   guitar

2 Let's learn our letters

 1 Listen and trace.

 2a Listen, point and say.

 2b Listen, find and say.

3 Trace and write.

4 ▲▲ Write.

5 Find and circle **G** and **g** in red. Circle **H** and **h** in green.
Then trace.

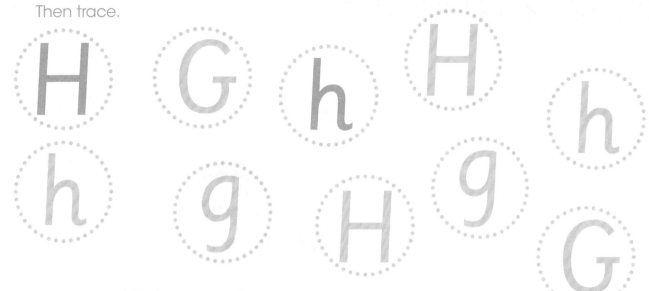

6 Look and tick ✓ **g** or **h**.
Then say.

7 🔺 Match and write.

hill   hand   house

3 Let's learn our letters

31 **1** Listen and trace.

32 **2a** Listen, point and say.

33 **2b** Listen, find and say.

3 Trace and write.

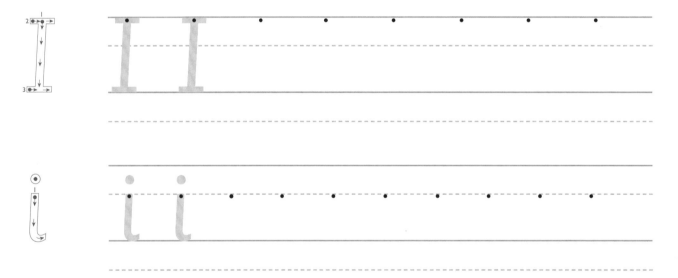

4 ▲▲ Write.

5 Find and colour **G**, **g**, **H**, **h** and **I**, **i**.

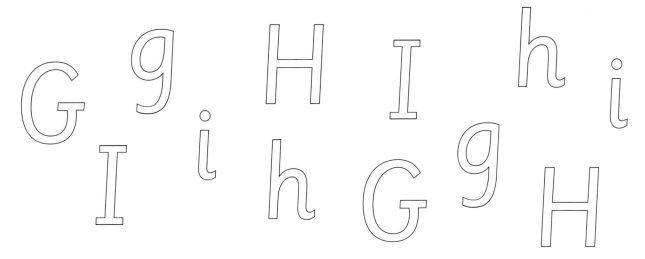

6 Join the dots.

Write **g**, **h** or **i**. Then say.

7 🔺 Look and write.

G is for _uitar.
H is for _and.
I is for _nsect.

4 Story time: Look!

 1 Listen and point.

 2 ⇅ **Listen, say and circle or write.**

The girls are hot and hungry.

Look! There is a house on the hill.

Look! There is ink on the ground.

Look! There is a goat in the house.

Look! There is an insect on the goat.

Meh-eh-eh!

3 The insect has a friend. She is hiding. Find her and colour.

5 I can do it!

1 Listen and colour.
Listen and write **g**, **h** or **i**.

2 Draw lines to match the letters.

G   i   **h**   **i**
H   g   **l**   **G**
I   h   **g**   **H**

3 Match the pictures that start with the same sound.

igloo   goat   hill

house   ink   girl

4 ▲▲ Say and write the words in activity 3.

1 Look, point and say the letters.

Then trace the big letters.

A

___nt

B

___oy

C

___ap

D

___en

E

_lk

F

___ox

G

___irl

H

___ill

I

___gloo

2 Look at 1 again. Write the missing sounds.

Say the words. Then say and write the missing sounds.

3 Say the sound and words.

Circle the odd picture out.

a

b

c

4 Find the letters.
Write and match. Then colour.

d

e

d

f

e

5 Say the words.
Then match.

frog

egg

fox

den

_ _ _

_ _ _

f r o g

_ _ _

6 ▲▲ **Write the words next to the pictures.**

7a **What can you see?**
Write **g**, **h** or **i**.

_irl   _oat   _ill   _ouse   _uitar

_and

_nk

7b Complete the words.

8a Look and guess. Find the letters and say.

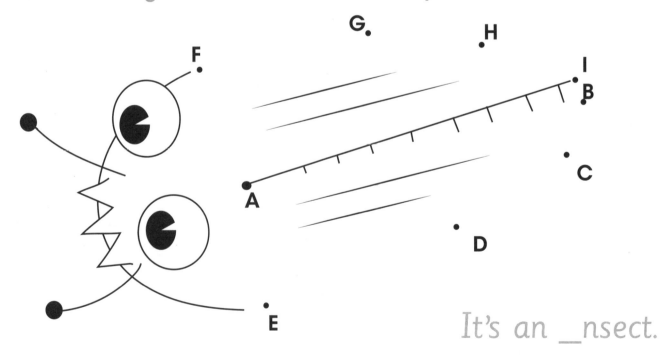

It's an _nsect.

8b Join the dots. Write.